FAMILY CIRCUS®

IT'S UP AND LET 'EM AT ME

Bil Keane

FAWCETT GOLD MEDAL • NEW YORK

The Family Circus
© 1991 Bil Keane, Inc.
Dist. by KING FEATURES SYNDICATE, Inc.

A Fawcett Gold Medal Book
Published by Ballantine Books
Copyright © 1991 by Bil Keane, Inc.
Distributed by King Features Syndicate, Inc.

All rights reserved under International and Pan-American Copyright
Conventions. Published in the United States by Ballantine Books, a division
of Random House, Inc., New York, and simultaneously in Canada by
Random House of Canada Limited, Toronto.

Library of Congress Catalog Card Number: 91-91893

ISBN 0-449-14619-7

Manufactured in the United States of America

First Edition: August 1991

"I'm not dirty. I just look
lived in."

"You have to be gentle when you bite
into a jelly doughnut."

"It's the piggy who had the roast beef!"

"Wanna be the first one to sign
my bandaid?"

"The sky's grumblin'!"

"Mommy! Dolly's kiss didn't work!
This still hurts!"

"Grandma! You have new windows!"

"We're here to shop, not to see
a movie."

"If you'll all be quiet, I'LL decide
which way to go."

"Mommy! Billy's goin' in there and
he's not old enough!"

"Oooh, look over here! A LAMP STORE!
Look at all the pretty lamps!"

"Where are your all-purpose sneakers?"

"Could we see your thumb? Mommy said
you must have a green one."

"Does this mall have any other rides?"

"It's a gas station for money."

"I have to go to the bathroom shop."

"Aren't you glad they have these
places to SIT, Mommy?"

"I guess we should have gone in there before having our ice cream cones."

"I wish there was a mall where Mommy
wouldn't meet ANYBODY she knows."

"Mommy, this shoelace lost its claw."

"I'd like 'Wheel of Fortune' better if
I could spell."

"Cats are smart. They don't grow too
big to fit in a lap."

"I wanna be a pitcher. You get a little hill all for yourself."

"Next year I'm gonna ask Mommy to pick
me up on the last day of school."

"Don't kiss me yet, Daddy. I don't
have my lips out."

"PJ and I are putting on a play:
'Snow White and the Dwarf.'"

"Put the tooth under your pillow, but
be sure you tell Mommy first."

"When Simple Simon met the pieman, did
he buy a pizza?"

"A man named Carl Sagan counted the
stars one night. He says there
are billions and billions."

"Make sure it says 'Happy Daddy's
Day' 'cause we never call
Daddy 'Father.' "

"The bell rang before I could finish
your Father's Day card."

"Know what I like about summer? We
don't hafta go indoors to smell
dinner cooking."

"The grass is flossing my toes."

"Mommy's making windows in the newspaper."

"We'll find a lot of them around
the trash can."

"Will you push us, Daddy?"

"Mommy, can I eat at Max's house if he
can get his mother to let me?"

"God always turns the lights down when
he's gonna put on a storm."

"Daddy's asleep. I can hear him purring."

"Skateboards are better than skates
— 'specially when you're heading for
the bathroom."

"The fireworks won't start until it's dark."

"My dad was 729th in the 10K run."

"You oughta come and see my haircut,
Grandma, before it's all gone."

"Are there butter SAUCERS, too?"

"How come he's wearing a seat belt when
he isn't in a car?"

"Mommy, if you'll give me some cookies,
I'll put an ad for you on my racer."

"Where's your 'Baby on Board'
sign, Daddy?"

"Kittycat is potty-trained real good.
She always uses her glitter box."

"Here I am at Mount Rushmore with four
Presidents looking over my shoulder."

"Mommy! These flowers are broken."

"People can fly like birds, but they make a lot more noise doing it."

"Come with me and see if you can find
ten things wrong with your room."

"And don't budge off that chair if you
know what's good for you, young lady."

"Why do they keep the snow up there
where nobody can use it?"

"I can't see if this tooth is comin' in. My eyes are too high."

"What's an aleck, Mommy? Grandma
says I'm a smart one."

"I think that might be God's fingernail."

"Kittycat is riding shotgun on your chair."

"My memory isn't as good as
my forgettery."

"Caution: low-flying aircraft."

"It's a yardstick. It's used for getting stuff out from under the 'frigerator."

"Don't mash the jelly, Mommy. I like
it in one big puddle."

"We've had five customers, and three
of them were Daddy."

"I'm colorizing."

"Oh boy! MUD!"

"Lakes are oceans with the waves
turned off."

"Do 'dog days' mean we buy presents
for Sam and Barfy?"

"We can talk to God anytime we want to 'cause he has a toll-free number."

"Hi, Grandma! Are childrens allowed
in these condominimums?"

"You won't hafta read to us, Grandma.
We brought our favorite video tapes."

"Grandma's backyard is just right for
you, PJ — tiny!"

"We should've left a trail of bread
crumbs. ALL these condos look just
like Granddad's."

"Because Grandma's dining room table
isn't big enough for everybody. Now,
EAT and not another word."

"This condominimum even has its own golf course, Mommy! Can we go lookin' for balls?"

"Why does PJ always get to pick out
his cereal first?"

"Grandmas are good at hugging because they've had years and years of practice."

"Grandma, do you think Mommy and Daddy
will ever be able to have TWO beds 'stead
of just one?"

"If you remember any scary parts from when you were little, Grandma, tell us when they're comin'!"

"Is it okay to tell Grandma Keane I'm
havin' a good time at Grandma Carne's?"

"You better be quiet or Granddad will
leave you out of the family history
he's writing."

"I can swim real
good already,
Grandma — watch!"

"PJ won't get out of Granddad's
swizzle chair."

"Mommy, what language is 'eeny, meeny, miny, mo'?"

"Know what souvenir I wanna take home
with me, Grandma? You!"

"Cindy doesn't have any brothers or
sisters. She's still single."

"I wish lettuce came in neat squares
like cheese."

"I have a headache in my tummy."

"I'm gonna put these shells in the
sandbox where they'll feel
at home."

"That worm didn't look good to
me either."

"If the Grinch stole Labor Day maybe
school couldn't open."

"Tape all my programs, Mommy."

"Look in this, Daddy, and you'll see church windows."

"It has four-wheel drive for rugs."

"Mommy's renting a safe-deposit box.
Now we'll never find the candy."

"Know where I'd like to have one of
these? On our sliding board."

"If Billy is named after you, why isn't
he called Daddy?"

"The trouble with playin' hide-and-seek
with Mommy is it takes her so long to
find us."

"If I traded a cow for some beans you'd
ground me for a week!"

"I hope today is one of the good ol'
days Grandma talks about."

"I'm sharpening your lipstick."

"This horse is doin' wheelies!"

"Why doesn't THAT organist ever play
'Take Me Out to the Ball Game'?"

"I get to sit up front near the radio!"

"I'm five today but I still feel four."

"When you read me my horoscope,
why does it always end with
'and be a good boy'?"

"And that's the story of Adam and Eve."
"Hey! That would make a good book!"

"Billy's usin' a guess towel!"

"How 'bout hanging some cartoons down lower where EVERYBODY can read them."

"I was tryin' to paint you a Muriel!"

"Jeepers, Jeffy, you picked a great
time to sneeze!"

"When we're not hitting flies with it
Mommy can use it as a sifter."

"I like your way better, Daddy."

"That's nice. They've reverted to pre-
electronic tag."

"Daddy, is this the birthday when we go
on social security or the next one?"

"Those little orange cones better get out of the street before they get runned over."

"Have we got much electricity left?"

"Wouldn't you see your dreams better if
you left your glasses on?"

"Did Daddy really send that letter to
the editor? It doesn't look like
his writing."

"Mommy's baking a lemon marine pie!"

"I need a bigger piece of paper. I can't fit the whole sky on this one."

"How about some LIVE football, Daddy?"

"When you turn this little wheel it
opens its mouth."

"Bend down here, Daddy, and get your
hug for today."

"Don't stop, Daddy. Sometimes my ears
stay up later than my eyes."